PREHISTORIC LIFE

INSECTS

CHRISTA BEDRY

WEIGL PUBLISHERS INC.

Published by Weigl Publishers Inc.
350 5th Avenue, Suite 3304
New York, NY 10118-0069
USA
Web site: www.weigl.com

Library of Congress Cataloging-in-Publication Data
Bedry, Christa.
  Insects / by Christa Bedry.
     v. cm. -- (Prehistoric life)
Includes index.
Contents: Introduction to insects -- Early history of insects -- A different Earth -- Adapting to change -- Finding insect fossils -- Studying the evidence -- Entomologists -- Insect groups -- Insect close-ups -- Insect life cycles -- Insect feeding habits -- Disappearing act -- Insects in folklore and pop culture -- Still digging for insects.
  ISBN 1-59036-113-X (lib. bdg. : alk. paper)
  1. Insects, Fossil--Juvenile literature. [1. Insects, Fossil.] I.Title. II.Series:Prehistoric life (Mankato, Minn.)
  QE831.B43 2004
  565.7--dc21

                          2003003969
              Printed in the United States of America
              1 2 3 4 5 6 7 8 9 0   07 06 05 04 03

Editor Donald Wells
Series Editor Jennifer Nault
Designer Janine Vangool
Layout Terry Paulhus
Photo Researcher Tracey Carruthers
Consultant Royal Tyrrell Museum of Palaeontology

Photo Credits
Every reasonable effort has been made to trace ownership and to obtain permission to reprint copyright material. The publishers would be pleased to have any errors or omissions brought to their attention so that they may be corrected in subsequent printings.

Cover: dragonfly, landscape (**Photos.com**); **Steve Brusatte**: pages 5T, 10, 23; **Corel Corporation**: pages 19 all, 25B, 29; **Martha Jones**: pages 15 all, 17BM; **Clarence Norris/Lone Pine Photo**: page 7L; **Photofest**: pages 24 (© **Paramount**), 25T (©**Walt Disney**); **Photos.com**: pages 1, 6R, 18, 20, 22; **PhotoSpin, Inc.**: page 21; **Photovault**: page 4 (**Werhner Krutein**); **Royal Tyrrell Museum/Alberta Community Development**: pages 3, 6L; **Tom Stack & Associates**: pages 5B, 7R, 11, 16 (**Tom & Theresa Stack**), 13 (**Chip & Jill Isenhart**); **Visuals Unlimited**: pages 12 (**Jeff Daly**), 14 (**Kjell Sandved**).

Contents

Earth's Greatest Survivors

◆　　◆　　◆　　◆　　◆　　◆　　◆

There are more insects on Earth than all the plants and other animals grouped together. There are insects that swim, insects that fly, and insects that crawl on land. Some insects eat anything they find. Others eat only certain kinds of plants, and some insects actively hunt for their food. Insects are found in all shapes and sizes. Some insects are only 1/100 of an inch (0.025 cm) long, while other insects might grow to be 10 inches (25.4 cm) long.

Crickets appeared about 360 to 325 million years ago. **Fossils** of crickets and other insects are rare.

Many of the types of insects that were alive millions of years ago are still alive today. Insects are good survivors because they are able to **adapt** to their surroundings. Insects have been able to

The dragonfly is a living fossil. It is one of the oldest living animals on Earth.

live in conditions that other kinds of animals cannot survive. Insects live everywhere on Earth. They even live at the North and South Poles during the summer months.

All insects have one thing in common. Unlike most animals, they wear their skeletons on the outside of their bodies, as a hard, crackly shell. Insects are air-breathing animals. Most insects have six legs, and they usually have two pairs of wings.

INSECT FACT

Insects are related to **shellfish** such as lobsters and crabs and trilobites, which were sea animals that lived between 200 and 600 million years ago. Hard, **external** skeletons are a common feature of all these animals. Animals such as the trilobite appear to be halfway between insects and shellfish.

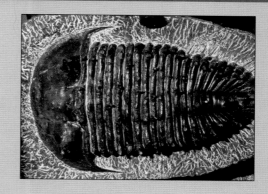

Early History of Insects

◆ ◆ ◆ ◆ ◆ ◆ ◆

Earth has a long and exciting history. For more than 3.5 billion years, it has been home to many types of animals and plants. Scientists have divided Earth's history into blocks of time called eras. The eras have been divided into periods. Different types of animals lived during each of Earth's eras.

PRECAMBRIAN ERA

Algae fossils

4.6 Billion to 545 Million Years Ago

◆ During the Precambrian Era, simple life forms first appeared in the seas.

PALEOZOIC ERA

545 Million to 250 Million Years Ago

◆ Paleozoic means "ancient life." During this era, more complex life forms appeared on Earth, including fish, insects, land plants, and reptiles.

Trilobite fossils

The first animals moved onto land about 440 million years ago. They looked like giant centipedes. These "centipedes" lived in the water, but some of them adapted to life on land.

The first insects were very simple. They had no wings, and they had basic life cycles that did not involve **metamorphosis**. As time passed, some insects began to fly. These insects had wings that stuck straight out, like a modern-day dragonfly. Next came insects that could fold their wings out of the way when they were not flying, such as the house fly. Insects that live in **societies**, such as ants and bees, were the last insects to evolve.

MESOZOIC ERA

Triceratops skull

250 Million to 65 Million Years Ago

- Mesozoic means "middle life." Dinosaurs and birds appeared during the Mesozoic Era. By the end of this era, many of these animals became **extinct**.

CENOZOIC ERA

65 Million Years Ago to the Present

- Cenozoic means "recent life." All types of **mammals** began to appear on Earth during the Cenozoic Era.

Saber-tooth tiger skull

A Different Earth

At the beginning of the Paleozoic Era, the large continent *Rodinia* split into smaller continents. The climate on Earth became cold. Toward the end of the Paleozoic Era, the continents moved together and formed the supercontinent *Pangaea*. The climate was warm, the sea level was high, and there was no ice at the North or South Poles. During the Mesozoic Era, Pangaea began to break up into separate continents. The climate grew moist, and forests became thicker. In the Cretaceous Period, 141 to 65 million years ago, the land continued to shift and change. The climate was warm, and there were wet and dry seasons. By the end of the Cretaceous Period, the continents looked much like they do today.

THE CHANGING CONTINENTS

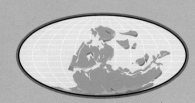  

Paleozoic Era
Rodinia splits into smaller continents

Paleozoic Era
Era ends with the formation of Pangaea

Mesozoic Era
Pangaea splits into separate continents

Adapting to Change

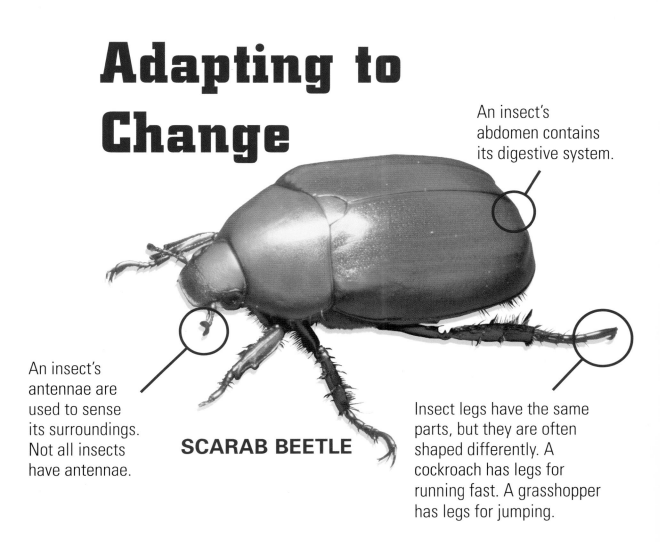

An insect's abdomen contains its digestive system.

An insect's antennae are used to sense its surroundings. Not all insects have antennae.

SCARAB BEETLE

Insect legs have the same parts, but they are often shaped differently. A cockroach has legs for running fast. A grasshopper has legs for jumping.

As Earth changed, insects adapted to fit into their new **environments**. Insects **evolved** on land, as did plant life. The first, simple insects ate the first, simple plants. Insects developed wings in order to escape **predators** and find new sources of food. Eventually, flowering plants appeared on land. Butterflies and bees developed to drink the nectar of flowers. Sucking systems, such as the butterfly's and bee's long tongues, evolved to get nectar from flowers.

Insect Fossils

◆　　◆　　◆　　◆　　◆　　◆　　◆

Many types of insects have been extinct for millions of years. It is not possible to go back in time to see them. It is possible to learn about them by looking at their fossils. Most insects died, and their bodies broke down into simpler parts. Some insect remains became fossils. Insect fossils can be compressions or impressions. Compressions are entire insect skeletons or parts of insect skeletons that were pressed between layers of mud and sand. These layers turned into rock. The insect skeletons and insect parts became fossils. Leaves with insect bite marks are left as impressions. Impressions are found in **sedimentary rocks** that were once layers of sand, silt, and mud.

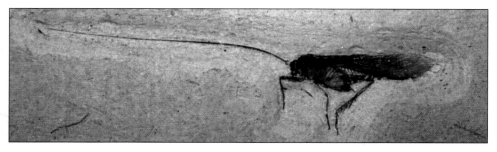

Grasshoppers belong to a group of animals that developed 600 million years ago. This group of animals includes a number of marine **species**, including trilobites.

Fossils are often discovered in the layers of sedimentary rock found in the badlands of North America.

HOW INSECT FOSSILS ARE FORMED

Many types of insect fossils have been found. Fossils are created when layers of mud and sand cover the body of an insect that has died. As time passes, layers of mud build up. The weight of the upper layers of mud pushes down on the lower layers to form solid rock. The insect remains become a fossil.

Insect fossils are not as common as dinosaur fossils. Insects are small, fragile animals that did not always last long enough to become fossils. Although insect fossils are not as common as dinosaur fossils, they have been found all over the world.

Revealing Evidence

◆　　　◆　　　◆　　　◆　　　◆　　　◆　　　◆

Scientists learn about prehistoric insects by studying fossils. Sometimes, one insect that has been partially swallowed by another insect is found in a fossil. Other times, it appears as though two insects were trapped while involved in a battle to the death. These types of fossils give scientists clues about which insects were predators and which insects were **prey**. Some fossils contain several different kinds of insects trapped with certain types of plants. This evidence suggests that these insects lived on or near these types of plants and that they probably ate these plants.

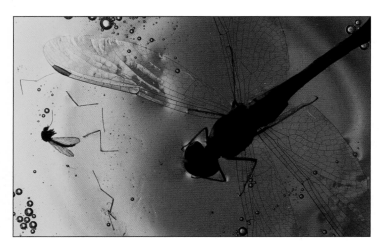

Most amber is 30 to 90 million years old. The age and variety of insects found in amber is limited because insects have existed for the last 400 million years.

Entomologists

A scientist who studies insects is called an entomologist. Entomologists help people understand how nature works. For example, certain types of insects are very important to human life because they **pollinate** flowers. Other types of insects may cause diseases or problems for trees and crops. Humans try to control the populations of these harmful types of insects. However, some methods of controlling insects are harmful to animals and humans. As a result, it is important to find safe ways to control insects. It is also very important to consider the **ecosystems** in which these insects live. Entomologists teach people how to keep insects under control without hurting other parts of the environment. To become an entomologist, you need to do well in science classes. You should also develop the language skills necessary for writing reports.

A job in entomology offers plenty of opportunity for exploration and discovery. An entomologist may travel around the world looking for new insects.

Insect Groups

◆　　◆　　◆　　◆　　◆　　◆　　◆

Insects are arthropods, which means they have hard shells on the outside of their bodies. Insects are related to clams, lobsters, shrimp, and spiders, which are also arthropods. There are two kinds of insects: apterygota, or wingless, and pterygota, or winged. Some of the insects that had wings in the past do not have wings today. They remain in the winged category because their prehistoric **ancestors** had wings.

Mosquitoes have changed little since prehistoric times. Today, there are 2,500 different mosquito species in the world, with about 200 species in the United States. New mosquito species are still being discovered.

APTERYGOTA: WINGLESS

The first insects to appear were simple animals without wings. The wingless, or apterygota, insects are divided into four groups: collembola, diplura, protura, and thysanura. The collembola are tiny insects that live in soil and leaf mold. Diplura are simple, six-legged insects. The protura are tiny insects that are seldom seen. Thysanura include tiny silvery insects, such as silverfish, that avoid the light.

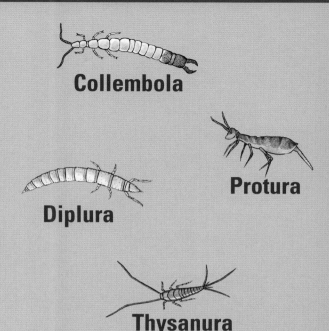

Collembola

Protura

Diplura

Thysanura

PTERYGOTA: WINGED

The winged, or pterygota, insects developed during the Carboniferous Period, 354 to 298 million years ago. There are at least 20 different groups of winged insects. The largest group is the coleoptera, which includes beetles. Cockroaches are part of the dictyoptera group. Meat-eating insects are found in the neuroptera group. Dragonflies, which have fixed wings that do not fold out of the way, are part of the odonata group.

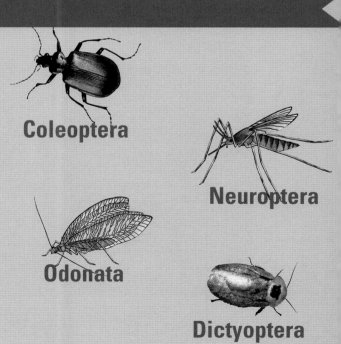

Coleoptera

Neuroptera

Odonata

Dictyoptera

Insects Closeup

◆　　　◆　　　◆　　　◆　　　◆　　　◆　　　◆

There are many different types of insects. Some insects can fly. Other insects can swim. There are insects that live aboveground, and some that live underground. Insects greatly outnumber all other types of animals and plants. Although it seems that there are too many insects, they all have a role to play in the ecosystems in which they live.

Dragonflies are beneficial insects. They help control mosquitoes by eating them. In some areas, dragonflies are used instead of pesticides.

BEES

- There are more than 25,000 species of bees; 3,500 of them are in North America
- Evolved about 135 million years ago with the appearance of flowering plants
- Most bees are social insects
- Bees talk to each other by dancing

CENTIPEDES

- Not considered insects by the modern definition, but they are the most ancient ancestors of land insects
- First insect-like creatures to come onto land about 400 million years ago
- Centipede means "one-hundred feet"
- Have poisonous claws to paralyze their prey

COCKROACHES

- There are 4,000 species of cockroaches
- Evolved about 300 million years ago
- Most species of cockroaches live in the tropics and are not harmful to humans
- The largest cockroach fossil was almost 4 inches (10 cm) long

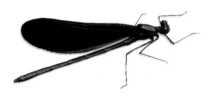

DRAGONFLIES

- There are more than 5,000 species of dragonfly; 400 of them are in North America
- Evolved about 300 million years ago
- Fossils of dragonflies have been found with 30-inch (76-cm) wingspans
- Dragonflies can travel 30 miles (48 km) per hour

MOSQUITOES

- Mosquitoes are slender and light, with very thin legs
- Have long, movable noses used to suck blood from humans and other animals
- Mosquitoes evolved 230 to 220 million years ago
- Female mosquitoes suck blood in order to lay eggs; male mosquitoes drink plant juices

SPIDERS

- Spiders are not insects because they have eight legs instead of six legs
- Evolved 400 million years ago
- There are 35,000 species of spider
- A 300-million-year-old fossil has been found that contains a spider almost 20 inches (51 cm) long

Life Cycles of Insects

◆　　◆　　◆　　◆　　◆　　◆　　◆

Human infants look like adult humans. Most prehistoric insects also had young that looked just like adult insects, only smaller.

Most ants live for 6 to 10 weeks. Some worker ants can live as long as 7 years. Queens can live for more than 15 years.

Other simple insects had young called **nymphs**. Nymphs hatch from eggs and often live in water or other protected environments until they are large enough to enter the world as adults. As nymphs grow, they gradually change shape until they look like adults.

A Special Life Cycle

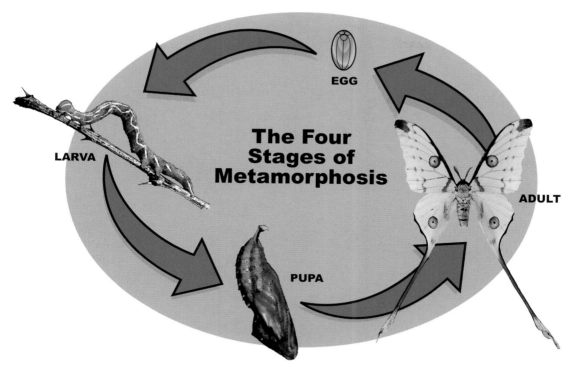

The Four Stages of Metamorphosis

EGG

LARVA

ADULT

PUPA

Some young insects, usually those species that evolved last, look completely different from the adults. These types of insects go through a metamorphosis in their life cycle. Bees and butterflies, which both evolved after flowering plants appeared on Earth, have four life stages: the egg, the larva, the pupa, and the adult.

THE DEVELOPMENT OF A BEE

The queen bee lays one egg in a room, or cell, of its own. A white larva with no legs hatches out of the egg on the fourth day. The adult bees bring beebread, a mixture of nectar and pollen, to the larva until it grows big enough to spin a cocoon around itself. After the larva spins a cocoon, the adult bees plug the larva's cell with wax. The larva develops into a pupa, which changes into a mature adult bee inside the plugged cell. Once it is fully developed, the adult bee chews its way through the wax plug and joins the hive.

Feeding Habits of Insects

◆　　◆　　◆　　◆　　◆　　◆　　◆

There are more types of insects than any other kind of animal, and there are just as many feeding habits as there are types of insects. Some insects peacefully poke around and eat the plants and dust they find along the way. Other insects set traps to catch food. Some fierce insects will hunt and chase other insects, including their own species. Most hunting insects can run or fly quickly to catch their prey. Some ants grow their own food to eat.

Sometimes insects cooperate with each other in order to obtain food. For example, ants protect aphids from ladybird beetles, which are commonly called ladybugs. The ants use the honeydew produced by the aphids as food for the plants they grow.

There are many types of beetles. Some beetles are meat-eaters, while others are plant-eaters.

Food Web

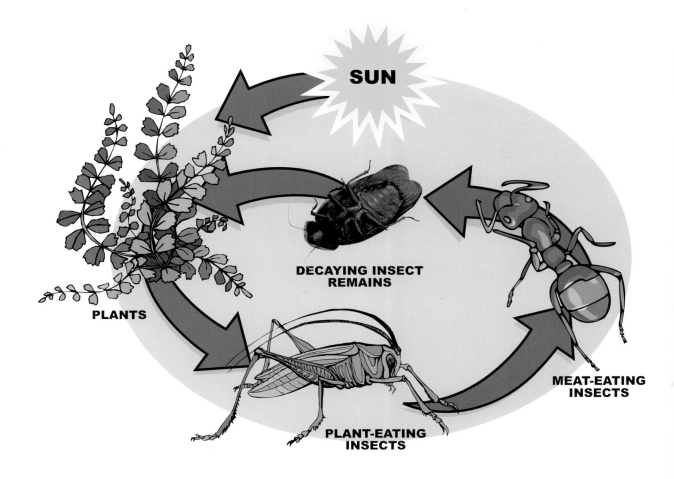

SUN

PLANTS

DECAYING INSECT REMAINS

MEAT-EATING INSECTS

PLANT-EATING INSECTS

FOOD WEB

Just like life today, all life in prehistoric times relied on an exchange of energy, also called a food web. For insects, this food web began with plants. The plants made their own food by converting the Sun's rays into energy. These plants were then eaten by plant-eating insects. The plant-eating insects, or herbivores, were eaten by the carnivores, or meat-eating insects. When an insect or any other living thing died, its body would break down and provide food for plants.

Disappearing Act

♦ ♦ ♦ ♦ ♦ ♦ ♦

Insects are survivors. Many people believe that cockroaches and other insects would survive a nuclear war. Insects are tough because they are very basic animals. For example, insects such as the cockroach have simple life cycles—they do not pass through metamorphosis. Because their life cycle is so basic, they do not require special conditions to survive. They are able to live on a wide variety of food, from fresh plants and meat to dust particles. Cockroaches have survived 300 million years of changes to Earth's climate.

Cockroaches can survive underwater for up to 15 minutes.

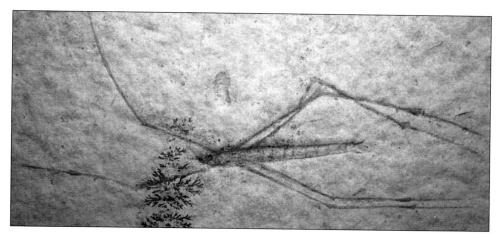

Water striders are at risk from drought. This is because they live on water and lay their eggs in water.

Other insects were not as hardy. A large number of prehistoric insects laid their eggs in water. The eggs hatched into nymphs, which grew larger underwater. There was a great drought 225 to 135 million years ago. The land became very dry, and many lakes disappeared during this period. Most of the insects that laid their eggs in water became extinct. These insects had no place to lay their eggs and no place for the nymphs to develop into adults. Entire species died out during this drought.

INSECTS IN AMBER

Amber is made when tree sap becomes solidified. Sometimes, ancient insects are found trapped in the sap. Many different species of insect have been found trapped in amber, and new ones are being discovered all the time. Most are perfectly preserved. Every hair on the body of these insects and the detail of their eyes can be clearly seen using a microscope. This enables scientists to compare prehistoric insects with modern-day insects.

Insects in Popular Culture

◆ • ◆ • ◆ • ◆ • ◆ • ◆ • ◆

Cartoon and movie creators are fascinated by insects and insect-like animals. For their size, today's insects can perform many amazing feats. Some insects can crawl up walls and walk on ceilings. Some insects can fly 60 to 70 miles (97–113 km) per hour. No wonder people try to show what these amazing creatures could do if they were the same size as humans.

Charlotte's Web, E. B. White's classic tale of a spider who saves her pig friend, was made into a popular cartoon movie in 1973.

The movie *Honey, I Shrunk the Kids* features ants and bees. Other insect movies include *Arachnophobia*, *A Bug's Life*, *Antz*, and *The Mummy*.

Spiders and termites have inspired the creators of cartoons and movies. Spiderman can jump from building to building, spin webs, and climb walls. Real spiders jump 40 times their own length. They spin strong webs to transport themselves and catch food, and they crawl straight up walls. Cartoon and movie termites devour buildings in seconds. Real termites chew up wood and plants to make their own buildings. They eat wooden buildings, but they do not eat entire buildings. Also, they certainly do not eat as quickly as they do in the movies.

THE ANCIENT WORSHIP OF SCARAB BEETLES

Egyptians have worshiped the scarab beetle for thousands of years. Scarab beetles are often found rolling around large balls of dung in the desert. People thought the balls  had eggs in them, so scarab beetles became a symbol of strength and rebirth. These balls do not actually contain eggs. Scarab beetles are worn as jewelry and used as decoration.

Digging for Insects

Every year, new insect fossils are discovered. This map shows some exciting insect discoveries.

The Florissant Fossil Beds in Colorado include fossilized redwood trees, insects, and plants. The fossils were preserved all at once, about 35 million years ago, when there were huge **volcanic eruptions**.

In 1993, a 313-million-year-old insect fossil was found in Kentucky. The insect is an extinct member of the palaeodictyoptera family. The fossil has traces of the original color pattern.

Fossils of trilobites in Rhode Island prove that North America was once joined to Africa and Europe. The trilobites in Rhode Island include several species that have not been found anywhere else in North America but are found in Africa and Europe.

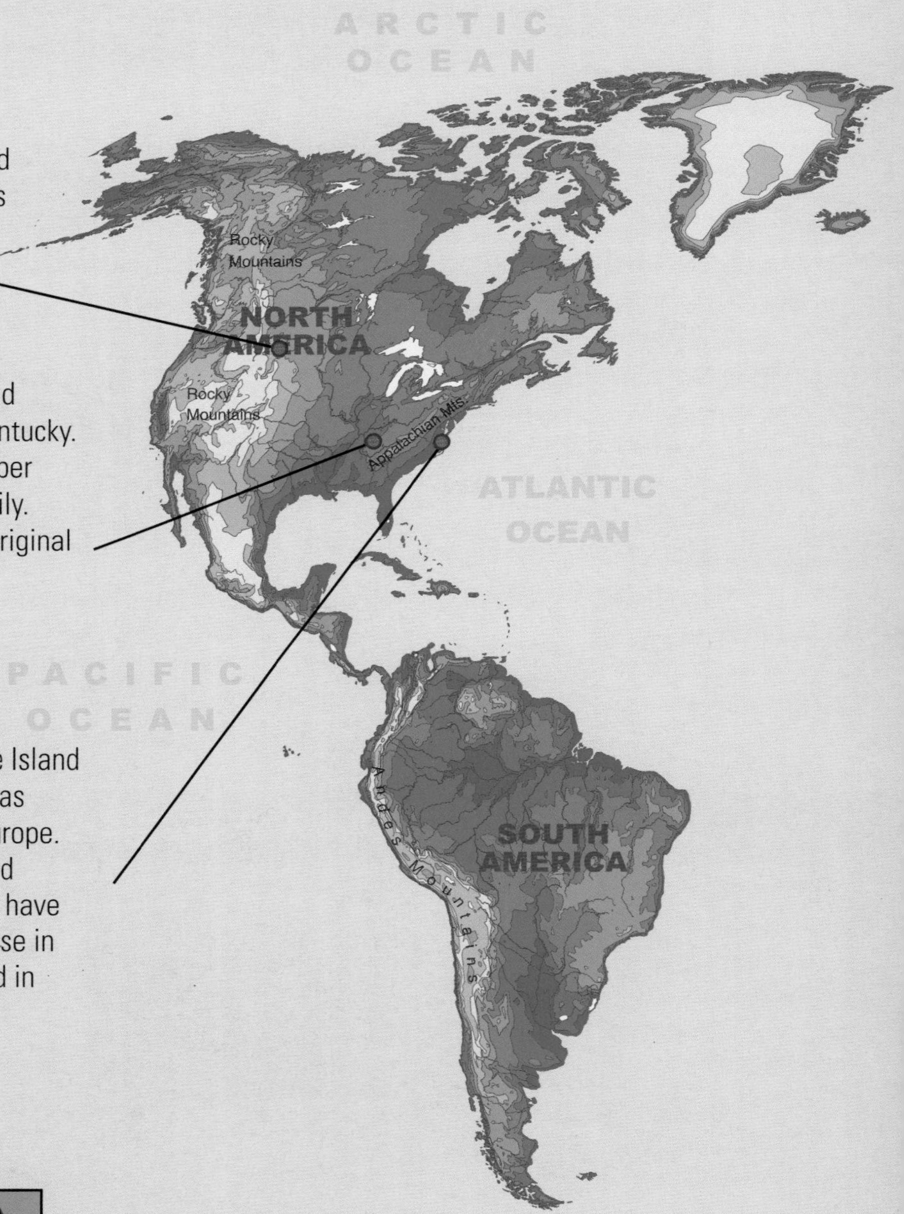

ARCTIC OCEAN
Rocky Mountains
NORTH AMERICA
Rocky Mountains
Appalachian Mts.
ATLANTIC OCEAN
PACIFIC OCEAN
Andes Mountains
SOUTH AMERICA

SCALE
621 Miles
1,000 Kilometers

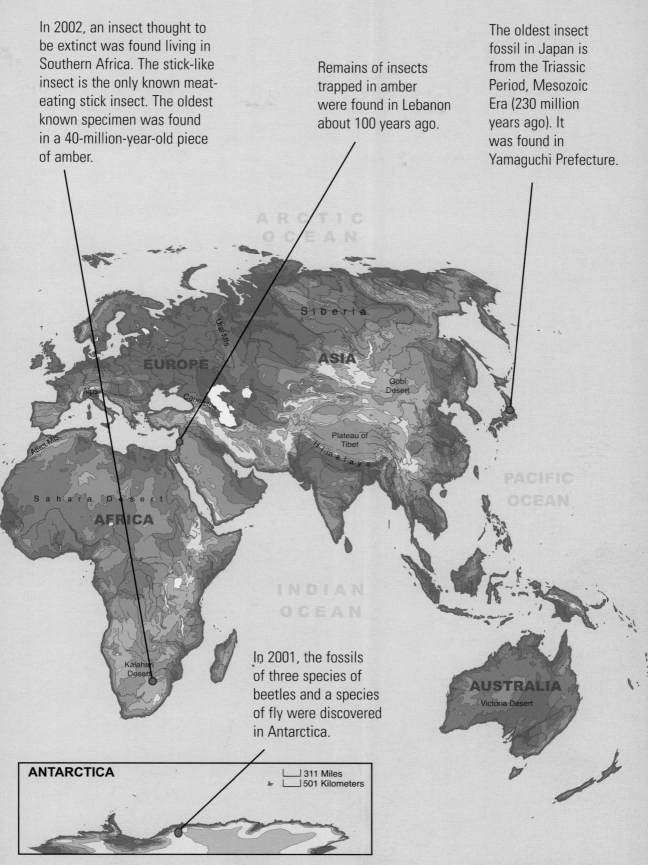

In 2002, an insect thought to be extinct was found living in Southern Africa. The stick-like insect is the only known meat-eating stick insect. The oldest known specimen was found in a 40-million-year-old piece of amber.

Remains of insects trapped in amber were found in Lebanon about 100 years ago.

The oldest insect fossil in Japan is from the Triassic Period, Mesozoic Era (230 million years ago). It was found in Yamaguchi Prefecture.

ARCTIC OCEAN

Siberia

Ural Mts.

EUROPE

ASIA

Alps

Caucasus

Gobi Desert

Atlas Mts.

Plateau of Tibet

Himalaya

PACIFIC OCEAN

Sahara Desert

AFRICA

INDIAN OCEAN

Kalahari Desert

In 2001, the fossils of three species of beetles and a species of fly were discovered in Antarctica.

AUSTRALIA

Victoria Desert

ANTARCTICA

311 Miles
501 Kilometers

Further Research

WEB SITES

To learn about the fastest, largest, and loudest insects, visit:
http://ufbir.ifas.ufl.edu

If you want to do science projects that involve insects, visit:
http://www.entsoc.org/education

To learn more about the prehistoric world in which insects lived, visit:
www.tyrrellmuseum.com

BOOKS

Discovery Channel Insects and Spiders: An Explore Your World Handbook. New York: Discovery Books, 2000.

Insects and Spiders of the World. New York: Marshall Cavendish, 2003.

Preston-Mafham, Ken and Rod Preston-Mafham. *The Natural World of Bugs and Insects.* San Diego, CA: Thunder Bay, 2001.

Tonnancour, Jacques (de). *Insects Revealed: Monsters or Marvels?* Ithaca, New York: Comstock Publishing Associates, 2002.

Ancient Activities

Buckeye butterfly

1 Create a cartoon character based on an insect. Research the special ability of an insect, and explain how this ability helps your cartoon character in his or her life. Perhaps you would like to make your cartoon character a superhero or a creature from another planet.

2 Make a butterfly. Take some heavy paper, and cut out and color a butterfly. Cut out a small hole at the top of the butterfly's head. Color a toilet paper tube like a cocoon. Take a pipe cleaner, and bend it to form the letter "V." Thread one point through the little hole in the butterfly's head, and twist it to look like antennae. Glue the butterfly to one end of a tongue depressor or ice-cream stick. Curl the butterfly's wings and slide it into the cocoon. Pull the stick to make the beautiful butterfly come out of the cocoon.

Quiz

◆   ◆   ◆   ◆   ◆   ◆

Based on what you have read, answer the following questions:

1. In which era did insects first appear?
2. What is the largest wingspan of dragonfly fossils?
3. When did social insects start to cooperate in societies?
4. Name three kinds of animals that are close relatives of insects.
5. Why did several species of insects become extinct about 225 to 135 million years ago?
6. Are spiders insects? Why or why not?
7. Name three ways that bees and butterflies are alike.
8. What is amber?

1. Insects first appeared in the Paleozoic Era.

2. The largest wingspan of dragonfly fossils is about 30 inches (76 cm).

3. Social insects started to cooperate in societies about 135 million years ago.

4. Crabs, spiders, and centipedes

5. There was a drought on Earth, and many insects that laid their eggs in water became extinct.

6. No. Spiders have eight legs instead of six. They are arachnids, not insects.

7. They both have wings, they both evolved after flowering plants, and they both undergo metamorphosis.

8. Amber is tree sap that has become a solid.

Glossary

adapt: change or adjust to meet new or different conditions or environments

ancestors: those from whom plants or animals are descended

ecosystems: the animals and plants living in an area together with their surroundings

environments: areas in which something lives

evolved: changed slowly over time

external: on the outside

extinct: no longer alive anywhere on Earth

fossils: the rocklike remains of ancient animals and plants

mammals: warm-blooded animals that give birth to live young, have hair on their bodies, and produce milk for their young

metamorphosis: a change, such as when a young insect changes into an adult form

nymphs: the infant form of an insect that will undergo metamorphosis

pollinate: moving pollen from one plant to another

predators: animals that catch and eat other animals

prey: an animal that is hunted for food

sedimentary rocks: rock that has formed from smaller rocks, and has been compressed over time

shellfish: a sea animal that lives inside a hard shell and has no skeleton

societies: groups of individuals that live together and cooperate

species: a group of animals that are similar and can breed together

volcanic eruptions: explosions of volcanoes that may cover a large area with ash and lava

Index

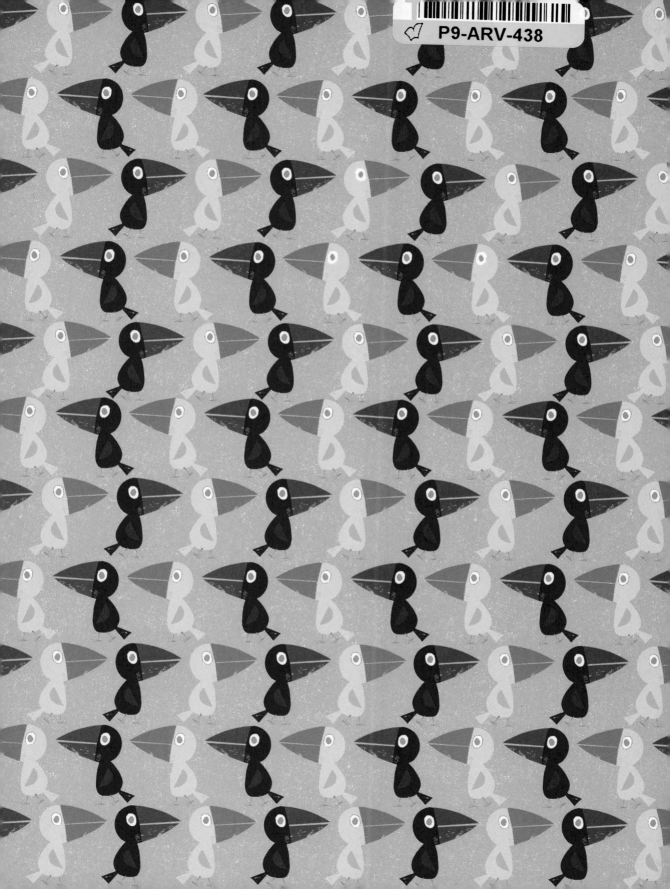

Britta Teckentrup

Oskar

and Mo

Prestel

Munich · London · New York

Oskar loves Mo
and Mo loves Oskar.
They are the best of friends.

Oskar would follow Mo anywhere.

Oskar and Mo have a favourite place
where they share all their secrets ...

... and they love to wear
matching scarves on a cold winter's day.

Oskar and Mo enjoy sharing stories.

Mo loves to listen to Oskar when he reads to her.

Oskar and Mo love to play silly games.

Building towers with Mo

is Oskar's favourite activity.

Oskar loves to hide and
Mo loves to find him.

Oskar and Mo sometimes fall out.

But they always make up.

No mountain is too high

for Oskar and Mo.

The night doesn't feel black

when Oskar is with Mo.

Oskar loves the way Mo is singing and dancing in the rain.

**Mo comforts Oskar
whenever he feels sad.**

Oskar misses Mo

when they are apart.

Oskar loves Mo
and Mo loves Oskar.
Who do you love?

© 2017, Prestel Verlag, Munich · London · New York
A member of Verlagsgruppe Random House GmbH
Neumarkter Strasse 28 · 81673 Munich

Prestel Publishing Ltd.
14-17 Wells Street
London W1T 3PD

Prestel Publishing
900 Broadway, Suite 603
New York, NY 10003

Library of Congress Control Number: 2017938210
A CIP catalogue record for this book is available
from the British Library.

Editorial direction: Doris Kutschbach
Copyediting: Brad Finger
Production management and typesetting: Corinna Pickart
Printing and binding: TBB, a.s. Banská Bystrica
Paper: Amber Graphic

Verlagsgruppe Random House FSC® N001967

Printed in Slovakia

ISBN 978-3-7913-7313-3
www.prestel.com

E TECKE   FLT
Teckentrup, Britta,
Oskar and Mo /

03/18

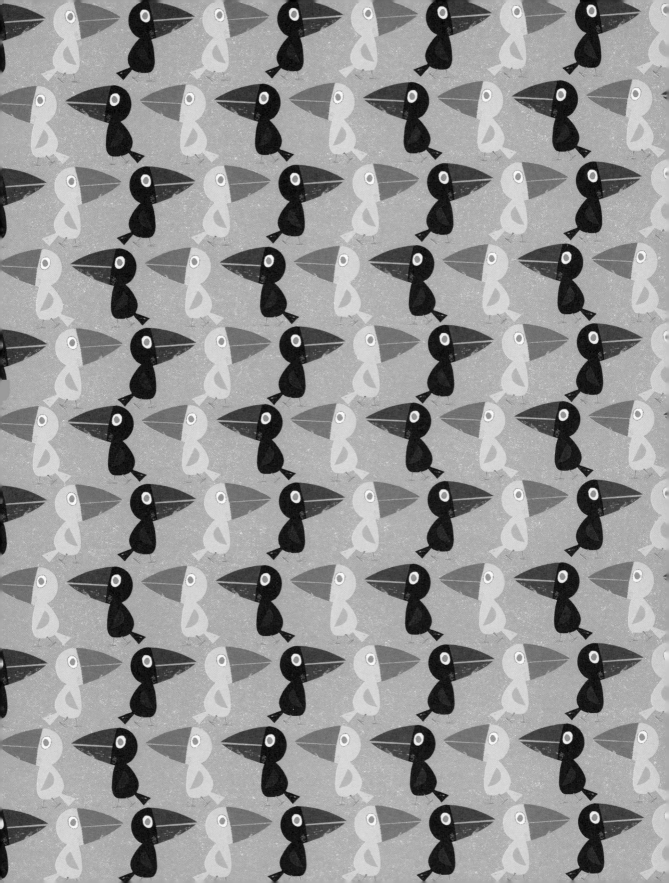